SISU

The Finnish Art of Courage

SISU

The Finnish Art of Courage

Joanna Nylund

An Hachette UK Company
www.hachette.co.uk

First published in Great Britain in 2018 by Gaia,
an imprint of Octopus Publishing Group Ltd,
Carmelite House, 50 Victoria Embankment,
London EC4Y 0DZ
www.octopusbooks.co.uk

ISBN 978-1-85675-380-7

A CIP catalogue record for this book is available from the British Library.

Printed and bound in China

10 9 8 7 6 5 4 3 2

Commissioning Editor: Leanne Bryan
Senior Editor: Pollyanna Poulter
Copy Editor: Jo Richardson
Art Director: Yasia Williams
Illustrator: Naomi Wilkinson
Picture Researchers: Jennifer Veall and
    Giulia Hetherington
Senior Production Manager: Katherine Hockley

CONTENTS

INTRODUCTION

"It's a myth. But it's also real.
It's a national icon.
It's a gut-felt quality."

What is *sisu* and why do we
need it? Discover the Finnish
quality of *sisu* and how cultivating
it can help you lead a life of
greater purpose and happiness.

WHAT IS SISU?
– an introduction

Sisu **could well be the favourite word of the Finnish people. Popularized in the 1920s but originating in the hazy past, this untranslatable term refers to a mix of courage, resilience, grit, tenacity and perseverance – characteristics that have shaped not just the fate of a nation but the individual lives of Finns on a daily basis.**

Finland ranks consistently high in international surveys of happiness. A small country of roughly five and a half million people, tucked away in the northeastern corner of Europe, Finland has nevertheless – in a quiet, understated way – made its mark on the world. You would be hard-pressed to find a bragging Finn, as blowing your own trumpet is considered extremely uncivilized. Ask a Finn what the secret to our success is, and you are likely to get a shrug and a mumbled objection to there even being one. But those who believe that it could be down to *sisu* are on to something. We are *secretly* proud of our *sisu*, you see.

So what does happiness mean for a Finn? Peace and quiet, order, independence, functionality and fairness all rank high, with "spending time in nature" being listed as a top happiness contributor in a recent survey. Finnish ideals are still coloured by a history of scarcity and having to tame a harsh environment. Which goes some way toward explaining why, in this age of comfort, many Finns still prefer their summer cabins to lack basic amenities (*see* page 46) and why we have a love–hate relationship with the climate.

Ultimately, *sisu* has a proven track record. Finland has built, and rebuilt, its future several times over. Looking at *sisu* as a guiding ethos in life, I believe it has much to offer us.

GROWING UP FINNISH
– our relationship to *sisu*

Like many cultural constructs that become ingrained from the start, *sisu* feels a little elusive. But how can we locate the defining thread of a weave? Where do you start? *Sisu* has been a well-kept secret for so long that unlocking it will take some close examination.

When I told a good friend I was working on this book, she said: "It's one of the most beautiful things you can say to someone, isn't it, that they have *sisu*. I still remember vividly the first time my parents said it to me".

AN INVISIBLE AND OMNIPRESENT FORCE

For anyone growing up in Finland, the concept of *sisu* is invisibly present everywhere. True to our national character, it is acted on more than it is spoken about. But there is no mistaking the place it has in our hearts. Some even argue that it is impossible to understand Finns and Finland without first understanding *sisu*.

Like my friend said, it is a highly prized characteristic. We credit *sisu* with giving us freedom and perseverance. On the eve of a race or an exam, parents encourage their children to look inside themselves for *sisu*. Being told you have it has the effect of bolstering it further, while feeling that you lack *sisu* has a correspondingly deflating effect on your self-esteem.

Even though it rarely gets defined, one thing is for sure: *sisu* matters.

WHAT SISU IS
– and what it isn't

The concept of *sisu* in the Finnish language is at least five hundred years old. In the most literal sense, *sisu* refers to the guts (*sisus* or *sisälmykset*) inside our bodies. It is thought to stem from the ancient belief that the belly was a location of strength (think "fire in one's belly") and the place where our determination originates.

SISU IS MANY THINGS...

The exact meaning of *sisu* is difficult to define. There's no one word in the English language with a literal parallel, and even in Finnish, *sisu* stands for a cluster of traits that includes stoic determination, hardiness, courage, bravery, willpower, tenacity and resilience. *Sisu* is an action-oriented mindset: it comes into play as you take on a challenge seemingly beyond your capacity. It is called upon when adversity and opposition force you to give up and only your courage allows you to hold on.

...BUT NOT BRAVADO

Finns have a reputation for being tight-lipped and stoney-faced. Ours is not a culture that expresses emotion very freely (although that is slowly changing). With this in mind, an essential trait of *sisu* is the lack of a need to talk about it. Any kind of swagger or talking up your bravery has no place in *sisu*. It's no good just saying you have *sisu* if you can't show it – let your actions do the talking.

YOU HAVE SISU
– now begin to explore it

SISU GLOSSARY

Sisukas: adjective, as in "you are full of *sisu*" = *olet sisukas*

Sisukkaasti: "doing something with *sisu*"

Sisulla: "by way of *sisu*"

Chances are, you have already tapped into your *sisu*. You just didn't have a word for it.

Let's be very clear: *sisu* is a universal trait. It may have been bottled and labelled by us Finns, but it is within reach of everyone. It lies within you, and you are very likely to have used it already.

Here are just a few examples of occasions when you may have displayed *sisu*:

▸ You ran the race to the finish line, even though those last few miles were torture.

▸ You decided not to give up on your marriage, even though the road to saving it was long and hard.

▸ You felt, in the midst of a dark moment, a surge of courage that helped you carry on.

But what else is there to *sisu*? Can it be explored and used as a strategy? Can it improve our lives? If the notion of growing stronger in *sisu* and learning to tap into it intrigues you, then this book is for you.

SISU SAYINGS
– from saunas to sweets

You won't have to look hard to find mentions of *sisu* in Finnish everyday life. With all its positive associations, *sisu* has undeniable commercial value as well as a self-evident place in our daily vernacular.

Sisulla ja sydämellä

Meaning "with *sisu* and heart", and originally the name of a Finnish film released in 1947. Now a widely used phrase, it describes the attitude we all aspire to.

Läpi harmaan kiven

Literally translating as "through the grey stone", referring to the hard, grey granite found abundantly in Finland. As an expression it means "with *sisu* you will stop at nothing".

Sisu, sauna, salmiakki

The three Ss that define Finland. We already gave the world *sauna*, and *sisu* could well be our next big export. Our favourite confection, *salmiakki,* is a type of salty liquorice. We're still waiting for that one to really catch on.

FACING LIFE'S CHALLENGES

From fighting impossible wars to showing the climate who's boss, Finns make use of *sisu* in a variety of circumstances. Whatever the challenge, discover how *sisu* stoicism can help you become more of an overcomer.

A SISU MOMENT
– when the going gets tough

We all have them. They might come early or late in life and their shape will vary, but all of us will face moments when we are presented with a choice: to give up or buckle down.

I call such times "*sisu* moments". There is nothing grand or heroic about them when they first appear – in fact, they are much more likely to inspire fear. Disaster, sickness, sudden unemployment, the loss of a loved one: these are things that we simply don't allow to happen in our minds, but they happen in reality.

Once the unthinkable has occurred, how do you go on? *Sisu* is for times like that. According to *sisu* expert Emilia Lahti (interviewed on page 147), *sisu* begins where our perceived strength ends.

One of the hardest things in life is having to face a challenge with no end in sight. It requires a completely new way of thinking and living. *Sisu* is for those situations when the odds are stacked against us and there seems to be no way out, or past, our present circumstances. Unlike daredevil deeds and acts of extreme heroism, however, *sisu* often goes unsung.

"Rather than the stamina to run up a mountain, *sisu* is the strength it takes to put one foot in front of the other."

THE WINTER WAR
– when *sisu* became world famous

The idea of *sisu* in its most practically applied sense was introduced to the world when Finland faced a challenging moment. In the autumn of 1939, the country was invaded by its neighbour, the Soviet Union.

FINLAND'S FINEST HOUR

The Soviets possessed more than three times as many soldiers as the Finns, thirty times as many aircraft and one hundred times as many tanks. Though the outcome of this *sisu* moment looked grim, it became our "finest hour".

There were more things for Finland to worry about than being outnumbered and short-supplied. The winter of 1939–40 was exceptionally cold. Temperatures as low as −43°C (−45°F) were recorded, and only those in active service actually had uniforms and weapons. The large numbers of reserves that were called up had to supply their own clothing.

The Finns had an advantage: they were skilled in cross-country skiing, and knew that the best way to counter the cold was to keep their dugouts warm and dress in layers. For the outermost layer they wore lightweight, white camouflage that made them almost invisible against the snow.

Throughout the war, Finland used speed, guerrilla tactics and economy of force to their advantage, working to isolate the numerically superior Soviet troops into smaller groups. The Russian soldiers grew to fear the "Finnish phantoms" that silently and stealthily moved through the landscape and made every bullet count.

SISU SUCCEEDS

In his book *A Frozen Hell: The Russo-Finnish Winter War of 1939–40*, historian William R Trotter credits *sisu* with the surprising, if not to say shocking, success of the Finns. He writes that the only thing the Finnish army possessed in greater quantity than the Soviets was their *sisu*.

SECRETS OF SISU
– what we can learn from the Winter War

DID YOU KNOW?
•••••••••••••
There is a war memorial in Suomussalmi, Finland, called "Open Embrace". It features 105 bells (*see* opposite), one for each day of the Winter War.

The Winter War encapsulates many secrets of *sisu*. It was the first time *sisu* was introduced on a global scale, and became a virtual case study in what acting with *sisu* could look like. The collective strength of *sisu* became a phenomenon to reckon with.

DON'T PLAY SMALL

It's easy to feel small in the face of large challenges. Instead, change your perspective and try to find ways of making your size work to your advantage.

THINK OUTSIDE THE BOX

The Finnish wartime strategy was about adopting guerrilla tactics and making the most of the home advantage. People were forced to come up with solutions for everything from food supplies to homemade mines.

DIG YOUR HEELS IN

People who find themselves in a war probably don't experience a sense of destiny. In crises we tend to focus only on keeping something bad from happening and we feel miserable, not courageous. Clenching our teeth and holding firm may not seem much, but it will win the day.

DON'T GIVE UP

When Winston Churchill gave his famous rallying cry of "we shall never surrender", he was rousing *sisu* in the hearts of the British. And so much of *sisu* is just that – in the face of impossible odds, stand your ground. *Sisu* is courage, but it's also a positive decision.

SISU FOR THE 21ST CENTURY
– what bravery looks like in modern times

The demands of the modern world are obviously different from those you would face in a war – great social skills, for instance, or the ability to sell a product convincingly. How we perceive challenges has everything to do with our own frame of reference and previous experiences. What is difficult for me might be a walk in the park for you, and vice versa.

In order to get a job, you probably have to go through job interviews – for some, a time of stomach-churning scrutiny made worse by the knowledge that your nerves really may ruin your chances. Or maybe you hate public speaking but are expected to give important presentations at work – something you dread doing with every fibre of your being. You might need to make a difficult phone call, or put on a brave face at the office even though your private life is falling apart.

Whatever the challenge, there are steps you can take to relieve your anxiety and tap into your *sisu*.

1. Prepare yourself

Hyvin suunniteltu on puoliksi tehty is a popular Finnish expression that means "being well prepared is half the job done". If you have to do something that makes you nervous, prepare as much as you can – and then some more. If your nerves start to fray, at least you won't have to worry about not knowing your stuff.

2. Care for yourself

In challenging situations we often neglect ourselves, or at the very least, put our own needs last. Rethink that and you'll find positive ripple effects reaching far and wide. Get enough sleep, fresh air, good nutrition and me time – you'll both feel and perform better.

3. Centre yourself

An essential part of being able to tap into your *sisu*, the inner strength reserve you have but may not be aware of, is silencing all the superfluous noise. Declutter your mind through meditation, prayer, deep-breathing exercises or simply spending some time in nature (*see* page 49). You'll be surprised at how clear and calm your thinking will become.

THE FINNISH CLIMATE & SISU
– testing our mettle

Several people I've talked to about this book have said: "You will mention the climate, won't you?". Indeed, there is no way that a book about *sisu* can be written without trying to explain the thing that shapes us Finns more than most – the weather.

Living in Finland means living with sharp contrasts. Daylight in summer varies from 24 hours up north to 19 hours in the south. Being light around the clock messes with the kids' bedtimes and makes the rest of us giddy with possibility and sleep deprivation ("It's only midnight, how about a game of golf?"). In darkest winter, at the other extreme, there is officially no daylight in the north (known as *kaamos*, the polar night – *see* page 31) and a maximum of six hours of daylight in the far south. Winter is long, and on rare days of sunlight, people jokingly ask each other if they've seen the "strangely bright phenomenon in the sky".

SEASONAL *SISU*

The rare Hollywood film that features Finland predictably shows wintry landscapes, but we do have four distinct seasons. Summer can be a fairly warm and stable affair without too much rain (note I said "can"). According to our meteorological authority, 25°C (77°F) is a "hot" day, which of course means that most summer days don't quite get there. But looking on the bright side, it's never too hot to be active outdoors.

Winter temperatures vary greatly, from several degrees above freezing to as low as –30°C (–22°F) or less.

The pristine white winters of our dreams, if they materialize at all, usually turn quickly into dirty brown pools of slush with a treacherous layer of ice underneath. It's hard to say what requires more *sisu*: blizzards on the way to work or months of greyness with dustings of wet snow.

EMBRACING THE EXTREMES

Autumn in Finland comes early and spring comes late, with both seasons having their own charms and challenges. But it is the extremes that rule our lives – from gritting our teeth and summoning our *sisu* at the approach of winter to celebrating the eagerly anticipated summer. Starting as early in the year as February–March, you'll see a devotion to the sun that most closely resembles cultic worship. When the first warm rays appear – snow still on the ground – people wrap up and go in search of a spot where they can sit well out of the wind, eyes closed, thermos mug of coffee in hand, basking in the sunlight.

Finns are generally a fairly level-headed lot, but there is nothing cautious about the way we enjoy spring and summer. We grab both by the horns and refuse to let go. Outdoor activity reaches frenzied heights, and it's considered a sin to spend a beautiful day indoors. Acutely aware of how fleeting summer is, we really can't be accused of not milking it.

NORDIC NOIR
– surviving winter with your sanity intact

It gets dark during the Finnish winter, and I mean *dark*. Between mid-December and mid-February, the country receives few hours of daylight. You'd think we'd be used to it, but human beings everywhere need light to function properly, and seasonal affective disorder (SAD) is very real. Aside from gritting our teeth and getting through it with sheer *sisu*, there are ways of making the winter months more endurable – even enjoyable.

TOP TIPS TO SURVIVE WINTER

1. Hibernate

Well, not literally of course. But winter is an excellent time to cosy up at home: light candles, gather round the fire, cuddle up under a comfy throw, enjoy warming and invigorating drinks, and generally spoil yourself a little. Have friends over for game or movie nights – winter is perfect for socializing at home.

2. Eat

This should come with a disclaimer, as a friend of mine said: "Come winter, it's all I can do to stop myself from shoving chocolate into my mouth with both hands". Not exactly a sustainable lifestyle, so try upping the cosiness factor with some hearty food instead – stews, for instance, and a full-bodied red wine. And light some more candles.

3. Go to the sauna

Ah, the sauna. The heart of Finnish life and an absolute lifesaver in winter, when its warmth will thaw your bones like no bath can. Finns go regularly, solo, with friends or *en famille*; most homes or apartment buildings have one, and so do gyms and workplaces. Make the most of it – you'll feel wonderfully warm and sleepy afterward, even without the beer that usually accompanies it.

4. Get out there

It wouldn't be *sisu* if we didn't drag ourselves off the couch from time to time, wrap up and go outside – even in semi-permanent twilight. In fact, getting fresh air and any available light is crucial for both mental and physical health. You'll thank yourself afterward.

DON'T BE SAD
• • • • • • • • • • • •
Light-therapy lamps are
commonplace on Finnish
desks. Just half an hour next
to one gives a much-needed
energy boost. Researchers
at the University of Oulu
in northern Finland have
even created light-therapy
earphones that send light
through the ear canal.

THROUGH ANOTHER'S EYES
– a foreigner's take on *sisu*

Englishman Joel Willans – author of *101 Very Finnish Problems* and the Very Finnish Problems Facebook page and podcast – lives in Helsinki with his wife Anna and their two kids.

"*Sisu* is a fascinating concept that I think of as dogged perseverance. Finns have needed to cultivate toughness. The climate is against them and their neighbours have either tried to colonize or invade them. The last famine took place as late as the 1860s – I've no doubt that having to survive on dried fish for six months shapes your worldview!

"I'm not sure I have *sisu*; I love comfort too much! And I'm not sure you see it so much these days, for the same reason. I like to say that Finns nowadays use their *sisu* to celebrate *Vappu* and *Juhannus* (*see* right). It's usually cold or wet, but everyone's set on having that barbecue or picnic because it's tradition, dammit!

"For Finns, part of their *sisu* is their high work ethic and idea of rolling your sleeves up. Take the summer cabin: you think you're going to relax, but before you know it you're chopping down trees and carrying boulders.

"*Sisu* is an admirable, positive quality that, to me at least, is bound up with struggle. What happens to *sisu* when life becomes too comfortable? I guess it remains to be seen. Then again, you can always rely on the climate to coax it out of you."

Vappu and *Juhannus*

Vappu (from the Swedish *Valborg*) is celebrated on 30 April–1 May, marking the arrival of spring. *Vappu* celebrations always take place outdoors, regardless of the weather, with abundant supplies of balloons, hot dogs and candyfloss on the last day of April and a traditional Champagne picnic on the first day of May.

Juhannus is the Midsummer celebration that takes place in June. Lighting a big bonfire (*kokko*) on Midsummer's Eve is an ancient tradition. It is usually lit on a beach and forms the centrepiece of Midsummer celebrations. Other Midsummer traditions revolve around eating and drinking under the midnight sun, even when the weather is less than ideal.

COLLECTIVE SISU
– not just for lone wolves

A PROBLEM SHARED
••••••••••••••••
Confiding in someone will not only make you feel better, it will strengthen your bond to that person. That, in turn, will open up possibilities for mutual sharing in the future, thus creating a positive circle of reciprocated support.

When we think of *sisu*, it's all too easy to imagine it as a lonely struggle. But that would be a mistake. *Sisu* may be an individual quality, but it's one we inspire in each other. What is true elsewhere is true for *sisu*: we are stronger together than we are alone.

The expression "No man is an island" has been repeated *ad nauseam*, but that doesn't make it less true. A person incapable of turning to others for help is to be pitied.

In Finland, too, *sisu* has often been taken to mean you need to hack it on your own – especially for men. But the old ideal of the macho Finn, armed only with his silence and *puukko* knife (the small, traditional Finnish belt knife), is dying out. Up until World War II, Finland still had a mostly rural economy; our industrialized welfare nation was built with an almost super-human collective effort after the war. It is our ability to work together for the common good that has brought us success.

ALL FOR ONE AND ONE FOR ALL

Sisu as a psychological construct really comes into its own when we are under pressure. A crisis in the family tends to turn the spotlight on its dynamics, whether good or bad. Whatever the challenge, choosing to think like a team will make a world of difference. In difficult times, we need to be able to lean on each other and subsequently offer each other that same support. Chances are, on days when you are running low on *sisu*, someone near you will be able to top it up again.

"Above all, *sisu* is a collective choice.
We are strong together."

Emilia Lahti, *sisu* expert

BUSTING THE HERO MYTH
– why strength and weakness aren't opposites

The most prevalent misconception in Finland is that *sisu* equals a lack of emotion. The climate, the hardships, the war – whatever factors have forged *sisu* in us as a nation, they carry within them an element of crisis. In crises, different rules apply and we attend only to our most important needs. What goes unsaid is that the fallout – our emotions, our grief – will have to be dealt with later.

But what if there is no later? Treating *sisu* as a constant state of existence is not healthy. As *sisu* researcher Emilia Lahti (*see* pages 147–48) explains, *sisu* is a not a place where we live but a place we visit. The need to talk about grief and traumatic experiences has become widely accepted. But until fairly recently, that wasn't the case.

THE PRICE OF *SISU*

Finland hailed its war heroes and championed the part each soldier played. But once the war was over, all focus was placed on rebuilding the country and moving forward. The trauma of those who had seen war close up was not dealt with. Leaving the past behind inevitably meant leaving the heroes to face their post-traumatic stress all on their own.

Of course this was true virtually everywhere at the time, as so little was understood about the life-changing effects of trauma. But we would do well to distance ourselves from such thinking today.

STRENGTH IN VULNERABILITY

What is a hero? An outwardly strong, inwardly dysfunctional person? Someone who relies only on his or her own strength and doesn't trust anyone else? Surely we can do better than that. The idea that solitude equals strength is slowly losing ground. As we come to see success in life as a complex whole, with family life and personal wellbeing playing as big a part as any professional achievement, this is a healthy development. After all, being strong enough to show your own weakness takes some *sisu*.

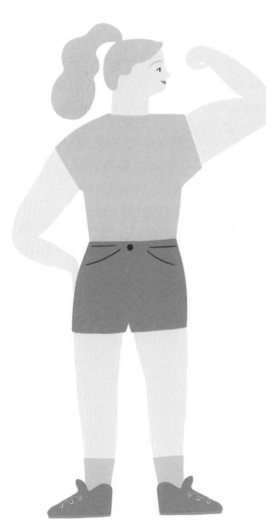

EXPERT SUPPORT
• • • • • • • • • • • • • • •
Truth is, most of us would
benefit from professional
help from time to time.
Simply having an impartial
person provide some much-
needed perspective can be
really useful. Schedule an
appointment with a counsellor
or psychotherapist – you may
find it helpful to see one
regularly, or perhaps just
one or two sessions will help
point you in a new direction.

WELLBEING
THE SISU WAY

Discover the role silence plays in happiness as you celebrate discomfort and try a little nature mindfulness *à la sisu*.

SILENCE
– it speaks volumes to Finns

Some joke that "Finns know how to be silent in several languages". Hilarious – and partly true.

If Finns are a people of few words, it's because we generally dislike babbling. Call it pragmatic, curt or just downright rude, we think over what we want to say and then say it – without any embellishments.

But things are changing. In the 1990s, Finland spearheaded the mobile revolution with phone giant Nokia and its "Connecting people" slogan. We've since grown increasingly chatty – at least on the phone. But foreigners are still likely to be unnerved by companionable silences that can sometimes last several minutes (and that's among friends). A British colleague of mine once agonized over the Friday afternoon coffee time that was coming up. "I just can't stand it! Everyone sitting in silence, eating cake. I get so stressed, I start babbling."

THE KEY IS IN THE WORD "COMPANIONABLE"

There is a sense that even though no one is speaking, we are sharing an unrushed moment together, devoid of social pressure. Once you get used to it, you come to appreciate the upside: you are allowed to relax. If you speak, fine; if you don't, that's equally fine, and we won't judge you for it – quite the opposite. It takes a wise person to shut up when they don't have anything of value to say.

We also have those awkward silences that occur after someone has said something inappropriate, but lengthy silences by mutual agreement are not awkward. That said, naturally there are differences within Finnish culture, with some Finns professing to feel equally unnerved by silences in groups as my British colleague.

"Finns view silence as a resource, not an embarrassment."

• •

SWEET SILENCE
• • • • • • • • • • • •
Don't let distractions intrude
on your precious moments.
Resolve to be fully present,
do not pick up your phone and
really observe other people,
taking note of small gestures
and expressions. Don't rush to
fill silences, and pay attention
to the uncomfortable ones.
Why did they come about?

INTO THE WILD
– why nature is so important

Geographically speaking, Finland is the eighth largest country in Europe, but it has a population of just five and a half million. This means that there are great swathes of unpopulated wilderness.

Two million hectares are nature reserves, and the "land of a thousand lakes" is home to more than 187,000 of them, alongside some 179,000 islands. And because ours is a large, comparatively empty land, it has a history steeped in silence, which also seems to have seeped into our souls.

BACK TO OUR ROOTS

Having the luxury of unspoiled nature makes us a nation of forest walkers, cabin dwellers and island people. The more I think about it, the clearer it seems: although we are modern people living in a modern world, at heart we are still rural. Even with the hardships it has brought us – or perhaps precisely for that reason – we love our sometimes harsh environment. It has given us our *sisu*.

DID YOU KNOW?
• • • • • • • • • • • • • •

Finland is home to a number of wild and often dangerous animals, such as wolves, lynxes, wolverines (*see* page 118) and bears, which means venturing out, in some forests at least, requires a considerable mustering of *sisu*. The brown bear (*Ursus arctos*, or *karhu* in Finnish) is one of Europe's largest predators and Finland's national animal. Finns have a soft spot for this strong but shy animal that hibernates during winter, only to emerge in spring with new cubs that it gave birth to while still asleep.

CELEBRATING DISCOMFORT
– essential to *sisu*

Starting in late June with Midsummer (*see* page 35), we collectively withdraw from our everyday lives and head out into nature. Spending three to four weeks with a *mökki* (summer cabin) as a base is the Finns' idea of paradise on earth. Many are lucky enough to have their own or share one with extended family, while others borrow or rent one.

It is there that we exhale after the long winter and enjoy the many hours of daylight to go swimming, fishing, boating... and generally lounging around in a slightly dishevelled state – "holiday beard" is a big concept for men.

A *mökki* you can reach by car is not as high status as one reachable only by boat. The lack of a road connection probably indicates that your house is on a secluded island, and that, in turn, means you have won the jackpot as far as summer hideaways are concerned. On the southwestern coast of Finland, even owning your own island is no big deal. There, locals talk wistfully of "getting away

from it all" at the summer cabin – most often located on an island even farther out to sea.

Although the rest of the year is lived out in snug houses (double glazing and good insulation, thank you very much), the *mökki* symbolizes a break from comfort. It will have a fireplace to provide warmth and cooking facilities, but rarely central heating and sometimes no electricity.

Running water is another modern convenience that gets frowned upon by the summer cabin diehards. Because squatting by the lake to wash your dishes in cold water is so *romantic*.

Something about modern comfort chafes at the Finnish ideal of self-sufficient *sisu*. Our ancestors grew resilient through the hardships brought about by farming the land. We uphold that ideal by retreating to the summer cabin for weeks on end, chopping our own firewood, carrying water and generally taking the smooth with the rough as we enjoy the long-awaited Finnish summer.

HELLO STRANGER
– getting (re)acquainted with nature

If you feel you are not exactly on speaking terms with nature, you're not alone. There may not be much of it around, or it may be hard to access. Or perhaps you're stuck in the rut of urban existence and wouldn't know what to do in the great outdoors.

There is one reason above all why nature is linked to *sisu*: it teaches self-sufficiency. Knowing your way around nature boosts healthy self-esteem, but it's okay (and advisable) to start small.

TOP TIPS FOR GETTING BACK TO NATURE

1. Think low key

Going for a walk, picking berries, skiing, biking, hiking – Finns tend to think of nature as an extension of their living room. Begin by making an effort to spend a little time outdoors every day, and go from there.

2. Think know-how

You can hardly be expected to love an environment you know nothing about. Read up on nature. What plant and animal species can you find? Which are rare; which are common? If there is a park nearby, find out its history and who designed it. Your strolls will become more interesting.

3. Think preparation

If you are a city dweller, chances are your clothes are more suited to pavements than pine forests. But you won't need to break the bank to make nature strolls a bit more appealing – *see* Take a hike, page 53.

MINDFULNESS THE FINNISH WAY
– turning to nature for peace of mind

Research shows that spending time in nature serves as a natural antidepressant. Long before systematic methods of meditation were developed, nature made us mindful – its effect on us is difficult to explain, but undeniable. It's where we go to centre ourselves and reconnect with a deeper source of strength.

Nature is a place of rest. It offers that precious commodity – silence – and the chance to hit pause on the constant din of thoughts and images that flood our brains. Like nothing else, nature grounds you in the moment – if you let it.

The following mindfulness exercises have been developed by the Finnish Association for Nature Conservation. Pick a peaceful place, ideally a forest or hillside, and give them a try.

RELAX AND OBSERVE

Find a nice spot to stand. In silence, take a moment to really observe your environment. Do you perceive something flying over or around you, floating in the air or moving in the undergrowth? Did you observe any of the following: a fly, a leaf, a mushroom, a bird, a cloud, a butterfly? Did you notice the wind stroking your face? Anything else?

HAVE A GOOD SNIFF AROUND

The memories we tend to remember best are usually connected to a smell. Close your eyes and inhale. Let your mind dwell on whatever associations come up. How does a certain smell make you feel? What does it remind you of? Take your time tracing that memory back to its roots.

FIND YOUR FAVOURITE TREE

Think about what kind of tree you would like to lean against when you need rest and rejuvenation. Find a nearby tree and touch it. What does it feel like? Now do the same with your eyes closed. What do you feel?

TAKE A HIKE
– some tips to get you started

Hiking is the perfect way to embrace the great outdoors and it allows you to enjoy nature at your own speed and fitness level. Since steady rhythms have a soothing effect on the brain, walking long distances also helps your mind adapt to the pace of your body, rather than the other way around.

1. Choose the right gear

Unless you're about to climb a mountain, chances are you won't need specialist gear. Sturdy, watertight shoes that are comfortable to walk in, a hat and lightweight jacket and trousers to keep out wind and rain will get you far. A typical rookie mistake is wearing too many layers. Trust that once you get going, the momentum will keep you warm! But do check the weather forecast for where you are going and dress accordingly.

2. Start small

If you're not used to hiking, try a short route to get a feel for it. Don't worry: your stamina (and enjoyment) will improve with practice.

3. Travel light

Many a walk has been ruined by trying to take too much along. Pack some basic provisions in a comfortable rucksack – water and light snacks – and perhaps a back-up jumper for warmth and a pair of gloves. If your bag feels heavy when you first put it on, imagine what it will feel like after a few hours!

Power snack for hikers
● ● ● ● ● ● ● ● ● ● ● ● ● ● ● ● ●
"Trail mix" is an energy-packed snack for longer hikes. Leave the chocolate bars at home and experiment with these tasty combos instead.

Go nuts: almonds, walnuts, peanuts, cashews, pecans and raisins.

Go savoury: almonds, pumpkin seeds and sunflower seeds tossed in onion powder, garlic powder and cayenne pepper.

Go powerful: goji berries, pistachios, dried blueberries, flaxseeds and dark chocolate chips.

Go luxurious: almonds, dried cherries and dark chocolate chips tossed in sea salt and ground cinnamon.

● ● ● ● ● ● ● ● ● ● ● ● ● ● ● ●

NATURE'S LARDER
– why foraging is the future

Finland has a lot of forest and the bounty it offers has always been there for the taking. With Nordic superfoods such as blueberries, lingonberries, sea buckthorn and the poetically named cloudberry, we are spoiled for choice.

Although you can now buy berries from the market, many people still prefer to head out into the forest, bucket in hand. The combination of fresh air and the small effort required to forage appeals greatly to Finnish sensibilities. Any way you look at it, foraging makes sense. We live in an age of renewed appreciation for locally grown, natural food. Foraging is also in line with the ecological ethos of "waste not, want not".

Foraging symbolizes a sense of self-sufficiency, a key aspect of *sisu*. Feeling at ease with nature and knowing what can and can't be eaten are empowering skills that were once passed down through the generations. After a lull in popularity, these skills are experiencing a renaissance.

TOP TIPS FOR SAFE FORAGING

1. Walk with a foraging expert
This will help you get to know your surroundings, what can be picked in each season and what not to pick with regard to toxicity and protected species.

2. Respect nature
It is important to ensure healthy regrowth, so avoid picking an area clean. Also make sure not to damage your surroundings or disturb animals.

3. Bring suitable containers
Plastic buckets with lids are ideal for berry picking.

4. Dress appropriately
Wellies are best for all forest outings, and depending on the area, you may also want to shield yourself from insects.

5. Know your area
Check out what rights apply in your locality. Are there areas that you need to avoid altogether? Also avoid polluted areas, such as those near industries and roads. Patches of forest or woodland are ideal; the more secluded, the better.

NETTLE SOUP

Young nettles are the most suitable for cooking, and should be picked in spring to early summer. Forage for your nettles at least 50m (165ft) from the nearest road, on a dry day and use a basket as a plastic container will cause the nettles to "sweat", thereby damaging them. Raw nettles sting, so wear gloves when picking and preparing them.

Serves: 4

2kg (4lb 8oz) freshly picked young nettles

1 litre (1¾ pints) water

15g (½oz) butter

3 tablespoons plain flour

2 chicken or vegetable stock cubes

100ml (3½fl oz) whipping cream

3 tablespoons dry sherry

salt

fresh bread, to serve

To garnish (optional)

2 hard-boiled eggs, shelled and halved

2 tablespoons chopped chives

Carefully rinse the nettles, and remove and discard any roots and tough stalks.

Bring half the measured water to the boil in a saucepan with a little salt. Add the nettles and boil for 5 minutes. Strain the nettles, reserving the cooking water, then finely chop them.

Melt the butter in a saucepan, stir in the flour and cook briefly over a medium heat, stirring, until a smooth paste forms. Slowly add some of the reserved nettle cooking water, stirring to make a smooth mixture.

Break the stock cubes into little pieces, then stir into the pan with the remaining reserved nettle cooking water until dissolved. Bring to the boil, stirring. Cook for a few minutes until thickened.

Stir in the nettles and cream, and heat through gently. Taste and season with salt if necessary and then add the sherry.

Ladle the hot soup into bowls and top each serving with half a hard-boiled egg and a sprinkling of chives, if liked. Serve with bread.

SPRUCE BRANCHLET ICE CREAM

The current year's young shoots of spruce trees (*Picea abies* or Norway spruce) are rich in vitamins and minerals. Almost neon in colour compared to the rest of the branch, they should be picked when they are 2.5–5cm (1–2 inches) long in the spring or early summer. Spruce branchlets can also be used to make drinks, syrups, jams and pickles, or simply eaten as they are.

Serves: 4

400ml (14fl oz) whipping cream

4 egg yolks

100ml (3½fl oz) honey

300g (10oz) young spruce branchlets, rinsed and patted dry

Safe sprucing

Since the foliage of yew trees is toxic to humans, it's important to distinguish them. Spruces have cones, while yews only have berries. Spruce needles grow directly from the stem rather than grouped together, and are three-dimensional, not flat, with many being prickly.

Pour the cream into a saucepan and slowly bring to the boil. Meanwhile, whisk the egg yolks and honey together in a bowl until pale in colour and thickened.

Slowly add the hot cream to the egg mixture, stirring constantly with the whisk until it is all incorporated. Pour the custard back into the saucepan and heat over a low heat, stirring constantly with a wooden spoon, until it thickens enough to coat the back of the spoon. Remove the pan from the heat.

Pour the custard into the bowl of a stand mixer fitted with the whisk attachment, add the spruce branchlets and whisk until smooth. Transfer the custard to a bowl, cover with clingfilm and chill in the refrigerator for a few hours or overnight.

Pour the chilled custard into a container. Freeze for 45 minutes, or until the mixture starts to freeze around the edges. Remove from the freezer and whisk vigorously to break down the ice crystals. Return to the freezer for 30 minutes, then whisk again. Repeat until the ice cream is fully frozen (about 2–3 hours). Alternatively, churn the custard in an ice-cream machine according to the manufacturer's instructions.

BLUEBERRY PIE

Makes: 6–8 slices
• • • • • • • • • • • • • • • •

150g (5½oz) butter, softened

200g (7oz) unrefined (raw) cane sugar

1 egg

250g (9oz) plain flour

200g (7oz) rolled oats

1 tablespoon vanilla sugar

700g (1lb 9oz) wild (sometimes referred to as bilberries) or cultivated blueberries, fresh or frozen, defrosted if frozen

dusting of potato flour (if the berries were frozen or are very moist)

whipped cream, vanilla sauce or vanilla ice cream, to serve

Finnish forest blueberries are abundant and increasingly popular for their extraordinary health properties. Blueberries are some of the most nutrient-packed berries in existence – antioxidant, anti-inflammatory and high in flavonoids and vitamin A.

Preheat the oven to 220°C (425°F), Gas Mark 7.

Place the butter, sugar, egg, flour, oats and vanilla sugar in the bowl of a stand mixer fitted with the paddle attachment and mix to form a dough, or place the ingredients in a bowl and use an electric hand-held mixer.

Add the blueberries to a 24cm (9½-inch) round pie dish or quiche/flan tin, dusting with a little potato flour if necessary, then crumble the dough over the berries. Bake the pie for about 25 minutes until golden-brown on top.

Serve lukewarm with a dollop of whipped cream or vanilla sauce, or a scoop of vanilla ice cream.

BLACKBERRY, BASIL & LEMON VODKA COCKTAIL

True to form, perhaps, Finns have something of an affinity with strong drink. Their oldest brand of vodka (first made in 1888) still uses glacial spring water in its manufacture. Berry-flavoured spirits are popular, with rare delicacies such as cloudberry and sea buckthorn adding an air of sophistication to any cocktail.

For the honey syrup, mix the honey with the measured hot water until it has melted.

Gently crush the basil leaves and blackberries using a pestle and mortar (or a muddler, if you have one, in the base of a cocktail shaker or mixing glass).

Transfer to a cocktail shaker, add the vodka, honey syrup, lemon juice and soda water, and shake for 15 seconds.

Strain into a tall glass filled with ice cubes or crushed ice, and garnish with extra basil leaves and blackberries and a slice of lemon.

Serves: 1

5 basil leaves, plus extra to garnish

10 blackberries, plus extra to garnish

1½ tablespoons vodka

1 tablespoon Honey Syrup (*see* below)

1 tablespoon freshly squeezed lemon juice

100ml (3½fl oz) soda water

For the honey syrup:

4 tablespoons honey

2 tablespoons freshly boiled water

slice of lemon, to garnish

ice cubes or crushed ice, to serve

BRINGING NATURE INDOORS
– the benefits of houseplants

If you can't come to nature, nature can still come to you. Houseplants are not only decorative but also bring some real health benefits into the home, as they clean the air and add moisture to dry environments.

PLANTS HELP US BREATHE

We inhale oxygen and exhale carbon dioxide. During photosynthesis, plants do the opposite: they absorb carbon dioxide and release oxygen. Plants thus increase the oxygen levels in our environment and essentially help us breathe.

PLANTS HELP US WORK BETTER

Research has shown that studying or working near plants can have a dramatic effect. As with being in nature, simply being around plants improves concentration, memory and productivity.

PLANTS HELP TO HEAL US

Researchers at Texas A&M University have tested horticulture therapy, in which patients are given plants to care for. Patients who physically interact with plants experience a significantly reduced recovery time after medical procedures.

MAKE YOUR OWN TERRARIUM

A terrarium is a miniature garden for your windowsill or coffee table, and a beautiful yet simple way to introduce a little plant life into your home. A trip to your local garden centre will provide you with all the items you need, and the process involved is quick and easy.

Fill the base of your container with a layer of small pebbles, approximately 4cm (1½ inches) deep.

Top with a layer of the potting compost, about 6cm (2½ inches) deep.

Carefully remove the largest plant from its pot (be sure to wear gloves if handling a prickly cactus) and gently tease any excess soil from its roots. Use the end of a spoon to create a hole in the compost at the back of the container. Position the roots in the hole and then pack the compost firmly around them.

Repeat with the remaining plants, working in size order from the largest to the smallest and planting forward from the back of the container. Be careful not to position the plants too close to each other.

Add a layer of sand around the plants, approximately 5mm (¼ inch) deep, and add some larger pebbles and seashells for decoration.

Position your terrarium so that it receives plenty of sunlight. Water the compost sparingly once every two weeks or when it feels dry.

You will need:

medium-sized clear glass container with an open top, such as a vase, pasta jar or fish bowl

small pebbles

potting compost for succulents and cacti

selection of small succulents and cacti (try different sizes, shapes and colours)

gardening gloves (to avoid pricking your fingers)

tablespoon

sand

larger pebbles and seashells, for decorating

NATURE HOBBIES
– some more options

If hiking and foraging aren't your thing, there are other nature hobbies that increase peace of mind while still boosting your oxygen levels. Any kind of nature experience is a *sisu* booster. Here are a few ideas for you to consider:

BIRD WATCHING

Twitching is an enjoyable and inexpensive hobby. The more you know, the more rewarding it will become, but you won't even have to leave your own garden to do it.

Get a field guide or do some research online to determine what species are in your area. Check out what the birds look and sound like. You'll have better luck finding and identifying a bird based on its call, and there is a number of great audio guides available. A pair of small, inexpensive binoculars will also help.

PLANT COLLECTING

Collecting specimen plants to preserve is equally inexpensive and rewarding, and you can choose to create a collection of plants from your local area using a plant guide (taking care not to pick any protected species). Flowers and plants can be pressed, either simply (such as between the pages of a heavy book) or following instructions to create a proper herbarium. Once pressed, they can be arranged and framed to make decorative pictures for your walls.

GROWING YOUR OWN EDIBLES

The perfect combination of spending time outdoors and learning about plants and their habitat. Read up on different soils, or ask an expert to evaluate what edibles could best be grown where you live. Salad leaves, tomatoes, squash and green beans are both tasty and easy to grow. If you don't have access to a garden, there are still many vegetables as well as herbs that can be grown in a sunny spot on your windowsill or in grow bags on your balcony. Being able to add an ingredient to a dish or a salad from your own little garden is an unbeatable feeling.

DISCONNECTING FROM IT ALL
– steps you can take to recharge

Even with a strong love of the outdoors, Finland faces the same challenges as other countries when it comes to constant connectedness.

Considering that peace of mind – as well as peace with yourself and your surroundings – is essential to *sisu*, 21st-century life poses certain challenges. With technology weaving its way into every corner of life, our high-tech nation (88% of the Finnish population has internet access at home, 82% a smartphone) is slowly beginning to question the long-term consequences of living life online.

Constant distractions, shorter attention spans, an increasingly sedate lifestyle and early-onset problems with poor posture and eyesight are some of the negatives. On this issue, Finland is looking to the future as a small country on the forefront of new technology, but also as a country with deep rural roots.

TOP TIPS TO HELP YOU RECHARGE

1. Truly disconnect

When you go out into nature, leave technology at home. By all means bring your phone for safety, but put it in your bag and resolve not to check it. (This may also prove a good indicator of how hooked you really are and whether some bigger changes to your lifestyle need to be made.)

2. Embrace the silence

Nature is a great vehicle for growing *sisu*, as it requires the courage to come face to face with yourself. Too often, we let distractions keep us from dealing with life. If you know deep down that there are things you have been running from, stop and see what happens.

3. Schedule alone time

Try to set aside some time every day – 20 minutes if you can, but even five will do – to do precisely nothing. Sit down, close your eyes and just breathe. Catch up with yourself. What is going on? What are you feeling? Taking time to centre yourself will enable you to better channel your inner strength – your *sisu*.

COMMUNICATE
WITH SISU

3

How can you communicate
with fairness and integrity?
Apply your tenacity to business
negotiations? Have more
courageous conversations?
Here is an in-depth look at
communicating, *sisu*-style.

SPEAKING WITH SISU
– an introduction

Finns famously find strength in silence rather than in words. Can *sisu* be a helpful attitude in communication? And if so, how would that look?

Speak when you have something to say; otherwise don't. That's the Finnish attitude to communication in a nutshell. We love a direct and humble approach, cutting out anything we deem unnecessary. Into that box generally goes small talk for the purpose of greasing the wheels, bragging, talking about yourself or your achievements and any kind of one-upmanship, especially in business.

ECONOMY OF LANGUAGE

In our private relationships, silence can sometimes prove a bit of a problem. *Mykkäkoulu* (literally meaning "school for the mute") describes sulking spouses who avoid speaking to one another for a length of time following an argument. This phenomenon is naturally not limited to Finns, but one wonders whether it might be applied just a little more often in Finland.

On the whole, however, Finns appreciate communication that is fair, direct and truthful – we just don't like to spend a lot of words on it.

"The Finnish work ethic in a nutshell: hard work pays off; loyalty should be rewarded; what you see is what you get."

SISU IN BUSINESS
– how Finns negotiate

Although Finland is a country known for its bluntness and lack of a small-talk culture, is there still something to be learned from the Finnish way of conducting business?

In the early 2000s, Jorma Ollila, then CEO of Nokia, became known for his "management by *perkele*" (*perkele* literally means "the devil"). This concept refers to an authoritarian style of Finnish leadership that stands in contrast to that of our Nordic neighbours, who are perceived as being just so... nice. In fact, the expression itself was probably coined in Sweden rather than Finland.

However, most Finnish leaders and businessmen distance themselves from the idea of management by *perkele*. Brusqueness aside, Finnish leadership is characterized by *sisu*, honesty, a certain modesty and leading by example. Perseverance, integrity and tenacity are elements of *sisu* that are deeply ingrained in Finnish business life.

If there can be too much go-getter *sisu*, there are also many positives to doing business with Finns. I spoke to a Swedish businessman with experience of working with people from all over the world who commented: "In business, every culture relies on its own strengths. I discovered long ago that when you find yourself in a tight spot, you need to call in the Finns. I've never seen any other nationality tackle a crisis like they do".

WHAT YOU SEE IS WHAT YOU GET

Finns value discussion, but want it carried out as efficiently as possible. Democracy rules, but consensus doesn't; there is an understanding that in order to get things done, we need decisive leaders who can be trusted to make the final call.

CONFLICT RESOLUTION
– from factory floor to Nobel Peace Prize

DID YOU KNOW?
• • • • • • • • • • • • •

Former President of Finland Martti Ahtisaari (*see* illustration opposite) was awarded the Nobel Peace Prize in 2008 "for his great efforts, on several continents and over more than three decades, to resolve international conflicts" (according to the Norwegian Nobel Committee). During his career as a diplomat and peace negotiator, Ahtisaari was appointed UN Special Envoy to Kosovo and actively brokered peace in Namibia, Indonesia and Iraq. He founded the independent peace broker Crisis Management Initiative in 2000.

For all its praise of individual strength, Finland is a nation of togetherness. There are over 70,000 volunteer-run associations revolving around hobbies and interests, with 5 million members – not bad for a nation of 5.5 million.

The idea of pulling together for a common goal is also strong in the workplace. It's an arena where tensions sometimes run high – after all, core values such as justice, equality and classless thinking come into play here. Finns take their work ethic seriously and expect this to be reflected in labour conditions and wages.

Trade unions have a strong position in Finland, with almost 75% of the workforce belonging to one. The International Labour Organization (ILO) has ranked Finnish unions as among the most effective in the world. Collective agreements are common and dispute resolution usually begins with negotiations at the workplace.

INTERNATIONAL EXPERTIZE

On the global stage, Finnish forthrightness and *sisu* are put to good use in mediation. Finland has been actively involved in negotiating peace in conflict zones such as Northern Ireland, the Balkans, Aceh, the Horn of Africa and the Caucasus. The Finnish love of straight talking plays a large part in solving conflicts through communication, both at home and abroad.

SISU PRINCIPLES OF COMMUNICATION
– top tips for straight talking

. . . .

Many cultures operate on the basis of a set of complex social and cultural rules. As a foreigner visiting a country with a significantly different culture to your own, you are liable to commit a number of *faux pas* despite having read up on cultural differences. With its straightforward culture, this is much less likely to happen in Finland.

Politeness is a key virtue, but it can also keep us from sharing important issues both at work and home. Communication inevitably suffers when things go unsaid. To get started down the road to directness, follow the pointers set out below.

1. Don't sugar-coat it
. . . .

Indirect communication often confuses things. Telling it like it is does not equal a lack of tact, but it can create momentary discomfort. Finns look at it this way: only by first stating the truth can we start to change things for the better.

2. Be a good listener
. . . .

Giving your partner the time and space to formulate thoughts is a sign of a respect. Don't interrupt or talk over someone – this is counterproductive and makes people defensive.

3. Don't pull rank
. . . .

Hierarchy for its own sake is pointless. It matters little that you hold a senior position if your ideas aren't up to scratch. Impress with your competence and show yourself to be an equal – this will inspire goodwill and open up whole new communication channels.

4. Weigh up your words and appreciate silence
. . . .

Unhurried conversations are less likely to produce misunderstandings. Also, you won't have to worry so much about saying the wrong thing.

5. Embrace integrity

It's probably not possible to underestimate the importance of integrity in Finnish life, in business and otherwise. Your handshake and word really mean something. Consequently, if it turns out that you have been less than sincere, you may find forgiveness in short supply.

6. Be honest

Not only are you welcome to list all your concerns and doubts at the start of negotiations, you are expected to. This provides an excellent basis for doing business founded on genuine understanding.

7. Don't dither

By cutting out complex social power play and ego-tripping, decision-making is more likely to be swift and to the point.

8. Avoid drama

Present a Finn with a crisis and watch the lack of an emotional reaction. Finns usually thrive on such *sisu* moments, when they are called upon to tap into their inner strength. The quickest way of alienating Finns in a business setting is to go all emotional on them.

HONESTY PAYS

A compliment from a Finn is sure to be sincere. We don't like our important words to suffer inflation. That's also why phrases like *minä rakastan sinua* ("I love you") are too precious to be tossed about lightly.

SISU & EQUALITY
– a short history

DID YOU KNOW?
• • • • • • • • • • • • •

Women have held all the highest political positions in Finland: President of the Republic, Prime Minister (twice), Minister of Finance, Minister of Foreign Affairs and Minister of Defence.

In order to truly understand any of the Nordic countries, you need to understand the importance of equality.

Historically, all Nordic nations have relied heavily on agriculture, and in order for families to survive this hard way of life, the strong working woman was an early Nordic phenomenon.

FINLAND'S LEADING LADIES

In 1906, Finland became the first country in the world to extend the right to vote and stand for election to all women. Today, Finland is a country where women usually work full time, and where women are most likely in the world to be able to participate fully in its political and economic life. Equality is seen as key to Finland succeeding as a nation. It's also valued as essential to good, straightforward communication in relationships and families.

TOWARD AN EQUAL RELATIONSHIP
– sharing the load

With generous maternity leave and a chance for fathers to take paternity leave, Finnish society wants to promote equality in the home. Equally valuing the contribution and *sisu* of men and women is very important to Finns. With both parents working, dads need to be hands-on, and this is reflected in everything from nappy changes to who picks up the kids from daycare.

Rethinking the running of the home is also important for another reason: it decreases tension and helps keep communication channels open.

For a more equal relationship, why not do the following:

1. Discuss the logistics
. . . .

What are your favourite/least-favourite chores in the home? Loosely agree who does what based on the rankings of each.

2. Talk about expectations
. . . .

Depending on what your home life was like growing up, you may have unspoken expectations of your spouse. Dare to think outside the box and explore more unconventional ways of doing things.

3. Analyze yourself
. . . .

Do you hold others to a different standard than the one you hold yourself to? Do you rank certain tasks or skills as more or less valuable? How is this affecting your relationship and your contribution to home life?

4. Express appreciation
. . . .

The logistics of daily life can be exhausting, no matter how equal your relationship is. Put a spring in your partner's step by noticing all the little things he or she does – and you will find that appreciation reciprocated in turn.

A TYPICAL FINNISH MARRIAGE?
– interview with Riitta and Juha

Keen to find out what communicating with *sisu* means to a Finnish couple, I sat down with Riitta Väkeväinen and Juha Lappalainen. Incidentally they are both communications experts with a background in journalism, have been married for 26 years, and have a son, Ilari, who is 14.

R: "The cornerstone of any happy relationship is respect. It is the basis of all good communication. Love means being the first to volunteer, rather than keeping tabs on who has taken the rubbish out more times this week. We don't think in terms of 'you got to do this, so now I get to do that'. We are a team – always in each other's corner."

J: "Communicating directly is not the same as saying everything that comes to mind in the heat of the moment. You must take responsibility for how you communicate. I completely abhor the idea that directness somehow means you can say unwise, hurtful things to each other. The starting point has to be respect for the other person, even in the midst of a heated argument."

R: "We have found a method of sharing the work in ways that suit us. We don't think in terms of 'that's a woman's job' or 'that's a man's job' – whoever is more suited to the task will take it on."

J: "Growing up, my dad was often in the kitchen and knew how to cook and clean as well as my mum. That kind of equality has always felt completely natural to me. Life becomes a lot simpler when you let go of expectations related to gender."

R: "For me, a life of *sisu* is a life without stagnation. We support each other as independent people who need to have a life outside the home, and respect each other's professional ambitions."

J: "To me, *sisu* means a certain kind of flexibility in life. It's making an informed decision and sticking to it, but not to the point where it just isn't beneficial any more. *Sisu* is the courage to change things when they have to change. And fundamentally, I think, it's the courage to like yourself for who you are."

R: "*Sisu* is accepting that you have to roll with the punches in life. Being able to adjust is definitely part of *sisu*. It's about more than strength."

"Strong people, like trees, might
break, whereas a person of *sisu*
may bend but can always pull
themselves back into place."

• •

SISU IN RELATIONSHIPS
– tips for healthy communication

Family, home, work, hobbies – in the juggling act of life, one plate that often gets dropped is the romantic relationship. Good communication is vital to keeping your relationship thriving.

1. Always show respect

Your partner is a hugely important person in your life, and how you communicate with him or her should reflect this. Abusive language, name-calling and insults have no place in any healthy relationship.

2. Don't keep tabs

Be generous. Give with an open hand. Keeping score and calculating who does more inevitably leads to mistrust. If both come into the relationship with a desire to give and appreciate what is given, these things take care of themselves.

3. Give each other freedom

Appreciate that you and your partner are individuals with a need for private space and hobbies of your own. Trying to control or manipulate your partner will only drive them away, whereas encouraging them to do things they love will also have a positive effect on your relationship.

4. Work from your strengths

When it comes to domestic tasks, forget gender roles. What matters is what works in your family, not how someone else has worked it out. And if traditional roles are those in which you both thrive the most, why change them?

COMMUNICATING WITH RESPECT
– the value of integrity

Communicating with *sisu* may mean standing firm in your convictions, but it's not a free pass to be inconsiderate. Finns place enormous value on integrity – having it yourself means not walking right over someone else's. For a more respectful dialogue...

Be an active listener

In conversation, regardless of whether the topic is heated or not, practise active listening. This means giving your full attention to the speaker. Listen without interruption and without planning what you want to say next, and provide appropriate feedback. Don't take a phone call, text or play a game when either of you is talking.

Be honest

As kindly as you can, always be honest. The truth may hurt, but it's vital to a healthy relationship. Disagree if you will, but remain respectful. Apologize when you make a mistake instead of coming up with excuses.

Be self-aware

Understand how your culture and background shape you. For the most part, misunderstandings occur not because of what was said but because of how one party said it. Don't assume that the other party understands what you mean.

Don't attack

Give "we" or "me" messages rather than "you". For example, say: "I feel like we haven't talked much lately" instead of "You have been distant with me lately".

Don't manipulate

Don't resort to mind games or manipulation. It's not wrong to be emotional; just understand the power emotions may have on steering the conversation. Ask yourself: is this discussion fair on both of us? Is it respectful of the other party's integrity?

LEARNING HOW
– Miss Polite turned straight talker

National communication norms are one thing; family norms can be quite another. I grew up in a loving family that nevertheless wasn't any good at constructive conflict.

Disagreements would arise but were rarely confronted. The only indication that all was forgiven was if one resumed speaking to the other after an evening of sulking. There is no reason why it was like this. But every family has unspoken rules that it lives by, and the natural thing is to adapt.

Aside from the sulking "strategy" (never a good idea), my toolbox was sorely lacking in conflict-resolution equipment. I knew how to be polite and diplomatic but not what to do with the anger that kept simmering underneath. My hope for healthy relationships rested on simply getting along with everybody, or only spending time with people who took the same approach of avoidance.

Real relationships involve conflict. We can tell which relationships are important to us by their ability to ruffle our feathers. After all, why fight with someone you don't care about?

FINDING MY OWN VOICE

I pity my first boyfriend, who bore the brunt of my inability to communicate directly. The relationship shone a harsh light on everything I lacked in that department. But here's the thing: I learned. Step by step, argument by argument, I slowly found my voice.

And in the years since, I've lost my fear of negative feelings and stopped judging myself for having them. I've also become skilled in fighting fair: speaking from my own perspective and respecting the other party while standing firm in my own convictions. Learning these skills has certainly improved all of my relationships, personal and professional.

Not surprisingly, the art of being firm but kind is my favourite expression of *sisu* in everyday life.

RESPECTFUL COMMUNICATION
– and the techniques to avoid

Unfair communication can take very subtle forms. In 1945, Norwegian psychologist Ingjald Nissen identified nine "master suppression techniques" – strategies to suppress others by manipulation or humiliation. Berit Ås, Norwegian politician and Professor Emirita of social psychology, later reduced Nissen's original nine techniques to five.

Maybe because of our dislike of hierarchy and love of equality, these techniques often feature in Scandinavian public debate and everyone has heard of them. Having someone accuse you of using a master suppression technique is never good!

THE FIVE TECHNIQUES OF ÅS ARE:
1. Making someone feel invisible by ignoring them – for example, not giving them credit or stealing their ideas.

2. Ridiculing someone – publically commenting on, or laughing at, someone's personal traits.

3. Withholding information from someone – for example, not telling them of a meeting, but still blaming them for missing it.

4. Double bind – punishing and belittling someone regardless of what they do.

5. Heaping blame – embarrassing someone or insinuating guilt.

The main point is understanding the dynamics of these techniques so that we can avoid them. This also applies to parenting – when a child needs to be convinced to do something, things can get ugly. Keeping communication fair and respectful can be a real challenge. Nevertheless, good communication should apply to everyone; nobody is too young to learn to communicate fairly and respectfully.

THE KIDS ARE
ALL RIGHT

Finnish children are exposed to *sisu* from the word go. Explore how *sisu* can help you raise resilient, happy kids, too.

EARLY EMPOWERMENT
– a sisu childhood

When I took my first wobbly steps on ice skates aged four, my mother was standing on the sidelines cheering me on. The ice was cold, hard and not very even, and I didn't like trying out new things. I wanted to leave. My mother smiled encouragingly, and as I shakily ventured out farther on the ice, I heard her shout *"Rohkeasti vaan!"* behind me.

This Finnish expression can be roughly translated as "Boldly now!" and typifies our attitude to raising kids. In favour of cheerful empowerment over wrapping the kids in cotton wool, Finnish parents seek to foster a can-do attitude that is based on facing and overcoming challenges rather than empty praise. This ideal lies at the very heart of *sisu*.

I never did become a very confident ice-skater, but if I ever have to step out of my comfort zone and do something that scares me, I still hear *Rohkeasti vaan!* in the back of my mind.

"Facing and overcoming challenges is key to fostering *sisu*."

PARENTING WITH SISU
– some basic guidelines

Sisu – courage, tenacity, perseverance – is something we all need. Are there ways of cultivating it in your child?

This poses an interesting question, as modern parental instincts lean toward shielding children from disappointments. Although done with the best of intentions, overprotection often keeps children "younger longer" by infantilizing them when they should be equipped.

And then we have the child-rearing methods of old, in the spirit of "throwing them in at the deep end" and characterized by a lack of understanding of the vulnerability of children and their need to feel loved, safe and protected.

Parenting with *sisu* lands somewhere in between the two. Challenges shouldn't be avoided, but children should be equipped to feel that they are up to the task.

1. Give realistic praise

When it comes to praising children's efforts, the Finnish approach is sometimes criticized for not being encouraging enough, but nevertheless the aim is to instil the idea that everyone's efforts are equally valuable. It's the difference between "That's the best picture I've ever seen" and "I can really see what you had in mind when you drew that".

2. Treat mistakes as a learning tool

Teaching your child not to give up at the first sign of difficulty is essential to fostering *sisu*.

3. Find enjoyment in discomfort

Wrap up the kids and take them for a walk in the rain, or go swimming even if the water is a little too chilly. Braving discomfort boosts self-esteem.

4. Encourage a healthy work ethic

Ask them to complete simple household chores like cleaning their room, walking the dog, regularly doing the dishes or taking the rubbish out. Being responsible for something, however small, fosters independence. It will also teach them the value of work and money. If you start them young, pitching in will quickly become a natural way of life for your kids.

LET'S GO OUTSIDE
– getting nature to co-parent

"What are you doing, sitting here? Go and play outside!" For anyone growing up with access to an outside area or garden, those are familiar words. Parents anywhere doubtless say the same. In Finland, however, this comes with the addition of "regardless of the weather".

Snowball fights, building snowmen or sledding for hours, with red cheeks and perpetually runny noses; playing in the rain and jumping in the mud; skipping with a rope, doing tricks on your bike, playing a spontaneous game of soccer with your friends or building a tree house. These are just a few of the activities that kids enjoy which don't require parents with bulging wallets. Another thing they have in common is a sense of joyful liberty. So what if the weather's not so great, so what if we get a little cold – we are having fun!

When I would complain as a child that it was too cold to play outside, the cheerful response would be "Just keep moving – that'll keep you warm!". Good advice, even if I didn't think so at the time.

NATURAL BENEFITS

If you dress your kids in clothes that suit the weather, it won't be difficult for them to love the different seasons. Also, kids are in any case more resilient than we tend to give them credit for. If something is fun enough, any discomfort can be overlooked.

Most importantly, letting nature play nanny to your kids enables them to find out things for themselves. Yes, they will fall; yes, they will get scrapes and bruises. But a reasonable amount of freedom is necessary in order for them to find their inner *sisu*. You can't find it for them, and neither should you keep them from discovering it.

THE BEST SCHOOL IN THE WORLD?
– education on the child's terms

When Finland has featured in international news over the past decades, the topic has often been our successful school system. The world first took notice in the early 2000s when the PISA (Programme for International Student Assessment) survey showed Finland topping the rankings in a number of categories.

Not surprising, perhaps, since education is highly valued in Finland. What grabbed headlines was that the countries sharing the top positions with Finland generally emphasized the need for tutoring outside of school and set school children plenty of homework, whereas Finland does neither.

GENTLY DOES IT

Underpinning our school system is the ethos that children need time to grow and develop. Finnish children start school relatively late, at age seven. They do get homework, but in primary school it should take a maximum of one hour to complete. The school day usually begins at 9am and has many recesses, and younger children finish no later than 1 or 2pm.

This gentle approach seems to work. Finnish children catch up quickly with their international peers, despite being "behind" initially.

WHAT MAKES IT WORK?
– secrets of the Finnish school

The Finnish school system frequently gets prodded for its secrets. Aside from a traditionally deep appreciation of education, the Finnish school rests on a foundation of strong values.

1. All schools are created equal

Parents don't need to jostle and compete to get their child into the "best" school, since public (state-run) schools offer the same high-quality education everywhere. Most children are simply enrolled in the school closest to home, which also means not having to spend much time on travel. There are few private schools. Those that do exist may run on a different ideology, but the level of excellence isn't higher, and thus, "getting ahead" isn't the reason for enrolling your child in one.

2. Teaching is considered a good job

In Finland, to hold a teaching position you are required to have a master's degree in your subject. This includes primary school teachers. Salaries reflect this requirement, and teaching is considered a respectable profession.

3. Everyone is entitled to a good education

Academically stronger and weaker children generally study together. Although this system is sometimes criticized for overlooking the exceptionally gifted students, it raises the achievement level of the academically weaker ones. It is up to the teachers to provide more challenges for fast learners, but to do so within the context of a "no child left behind" policy.

4. Children get individual support

When a child has learning difficulties, support is provided at an early stage. This might take the form of one-on-one tutoring with the teacher or a classroom assistant. Every mid-sized to large school has one or more teachers who are specially trained in teaching children with different special needs.

5. Teachers are trusted to teach

Rather than constantly evaluate and measure the teacher's work based on results, teachers in Finland generally enjoy a certain amount of freedom in the classroom. Although everyone follows a curriculum, teachers are encouraged to take a creative approach to teaching based on their own personality.

WHAT'S NEXT FOR THE FINNISH SCHOOL?

The latest teaching reform in Finland, only now being implemented, is groundbreaking – and somewhat controversial. The move is toward removing the boundaries between subjects to provide more synergy, while relying heavily on digital tools in teaching. Whether or not these measures can help create an even more successful school remains to be seen; there are those who argue this will better equip the next generation for an ever-changing job market, while others fear that academic excellence will be compromised.

ANNIKA LUTHER, TEACHER
– on imparting *sisu* to the next generation

Annika Luther is a biology teacher, author and mother of eight grown-up children. She teaches upper secondary school (16 to 19-year-olds) and lives with her husband in downtown Helsinki.

"More than anything, *sisu* is taught by example. That's where schools have an important role to play. As teachers, we role model certain attitudes, whether we are aware of it or not. I'm very concerned about the environment, but I want to remain optimistic. Optimism has the power to inspire. If you believe that nothing can be done, you won't even try. Young people run the risk of becoming disillusioned and blasé about everything they see happening in the world. It's vital that we show them not to give up but to push on; to fight for the things that we care about.

"As a teacher, what I want to impart is a sense of the common good. We don't live just for ourselves, but to care for our fellow man. We build this life together, and the sooner we learn to see that, the better.

"One of the best things we can offer children is our adult perspective. When you've been around for a while, you know that things always go up and down. Even though a situation looks bleak today, it can – and often does – change very quickly. Teaching *sisu* by example is also about imparting that wisdom. There is no need to panic; just hold on and keep pushing!"

STICKING UP FOR YOUR FRIENDS
– how *sisu* helps combat bullying

Sometimes we need courage to defend those who can't defend themselves. Cultivating *sisu* in your children means teaching them to think for themselves and not go with the flow.

Sisu is an individual capacity, but we use it for the good of the collective. As an individual trait, *sisu* is akin to having backbone. It really helps in those times when we have to go it alone.

DARING TO BE DIFFERENT

Every parent knows the importance of teaching independent thinking. The old adage "if your friend jumped from a bridge, would you jump too?" shows how enormous peer pressure can be. Rather than stand out, children want to fit in. Being different is not desirable but dangerous. To challenge a child to think independently at a time when friends are more important than ever can be just that, a challenge.

However, keep in mind that children have natural courage, which usually only needs a little coaxing to assert itself. Heroes are important, as are adults setting a good example. Children have a built-in sense of fairness. Teaching them to look out for each other is to believe them capable of making a difference, that they will rise to the challenge.

DID YOU KNOW?
· · · · · · · · · · · · ·
KiVa is an anti-bullying programme developed in Finland and in use by 90% of schools. Due to its high success rate, it's also being implemented in other countries. KiVa was based on decades of studying the mechanics of bullying, and addresses the issue from every side.

A SENSE OF JUSTICE
– fostering integrity

Children's rights are highly respected in Finland, where all forms of corporal punishment are prohibited by law.

Like elsewhere in the Nordic countries, the no-smacking ethos is strongly upheld. Not smacking your child is about more than not using superior force against someone smaller and weaker; it's about the notion that violence begets violence. It's also about acknowledging and protecting the integrity of children – the underlying logic being that those who have been treated with integrity will, in turn, treat others in the same way. Having integrity is to have *sisu*.

ALL TOGETHER NOW

Finland is proud of its social equality. Comparatively high taxes ensure a social security safety net for all in case of unemployment or illness, and education is free at all levels. It's not a perfect system, but it is powered by goodwill and the sense that we succeed or fail *together*.

Even in this age of individualism, there is a deeply felt sense of us working together to create a society we want to live in. Having *sisu* means treating everybody, adults and children, equally and fairly – an important value to pass on to the next generation.

ODE TO DISCOMFORT
– getting your hands dirty

Finns secretly love discomfort. The climate has been our primary adversary and we continue to triumph over it, quietly and persistently, by not letting it stop us from doing what we want – an attitude we pass down to our children.

Brisk cheerfulness is the best attitude to adopt regarding nature's more uncomfortable aspects. The global youth organization 4-H, which initially focused on passing on agricultural skills to the next generation, has a firm foothold in Finland. So does Scouting – a strong advocate of learning nature skills and braving discomfort. Schools also take some classes outside, for example by going on forest hikes to learn about plants. If you want your kids to grow *sisukas* (full of *sisu*), help them along with the following activities:

1. Enrol them in a nature club

They might find new interests and like-minded friends to pursue them with.

2. Go on a family camping trip

Your own example speaks volumes, and habits established in childhood often follow us through life.

3. Trust them with some exploring

Let them go on planned excursions on their own in safe environments. They will have great fun, and their courage will be bolstered.

DID YOU KNOW?
• • • • • • • • • • • • • •
In Finland, you can get a vocational degree as a wilderness guide. Studies include everything from leadership training and survival skills to kayaking, climbing and ice-skating.

SISU KIDS
– lots of fresh air and little fuss

We have some strange habits here in the Nordic countries. We let our babies nap outside in their prams – even in temperatures below freezing. We often sleep with a window slightly ajar right through winter. We like to give our houses a good *tuuletus* (ventilation) several times a day. And we let the kids play outside almost no matter what. All this stems from a cheerful attitude to things that foster *sisu* resilience and an ethos of "little fuss, lots of common sense".

Foreigners are regularly shocked at the pram thing. But, with sufficient protection, the cold can be exceedingly good for you. Fresh air makes you sleep wonderfully well and boosts the immune system.

HERITAGE OF HARDINESS

You won't see Finns go overboard with germ hysteria and applying antibacterial spray to every imaginable surface. There is no reason to take unnecessary risks, but equally no need to exaggerate potential hazards. The hardiness of previous generations is still ingrained in us to some degree. "Let the kids play in the mud and eat a little sand or snow; a little will do no harm!" (although "don't eat the yellow snow" is one warning that Finnish kids usually do hear in wintertime!).

I grew up on the south coast of Finland, where winters are generally milder than in the north. However, one winter in the 1980s was exceptionally cold – temperatures dropped to −33°C (−27°F) for weeks.

As usual, I walked to school. Kitted out in triple layers of underclothes and double mittens, two beanies and a scarf to cover my face, it felt a little exhilarating. At school, the really exceptional thing was that we weren't allowed to go out for recess. This was unheard of, since we would all be traipsing out for 15 minutes at a time if the temperature was, say, a more normal −20°C (−4°F).

My point? Once you've braved the elements, it's not that bad. And with a little cheerful encouragement from you, your kids will feel the same.

GET MOVING WITH SISU

From setting goals to jumping into icy water, take inspiration from some famous Finns with truckloads of *sisu*.

CULTIVATING ENDURANCE
– how to overcome the conditions

Considering that Finland is wrapped in semi-darkness from November to February and winter temperatures can drop to −25°C (−13°F) and below, Finns are surprisingly outdoorsy. Even in the snow you'll find people cycling to work. Sports are a pastime for the many rather than a hobby for the elite few, and ice fishing and winter bathing display a devil-may-care attitude to the elements.

This attitude has a lot to do with the fact that if we let the climate decide, we probably wouldn't do very much at all. But there is no denying that we genuinely enjoy moving about – almost regardless of the weather.

Sharp contrasts between darkness and light are typical of Nordic life (*see* page 28). Throw wind, sleet, snow and rain into the mix, and you'll understand why the climate plays a big part in our *sisu*. The key to cultivating endurance is a question: do you rule the conditions, or do they rule you?

"On the other side of endurance, joy waits."

FINNS & SPORTS
– a passionate affair

Finns love participating in sports, but we sure love watching it, too. So much so that we have invented a term for the sport of passionate fandom: *penkkiurheilu* (literally meaning "bench sports"). Whether practised from the sidelines or in front of the TV in your underwear, what matters is giving it your all.

We are in our element in traditional winter sports such as hockey and skiing, but Finns' interest in sports is wide-ranging. "Silent Finns driving fast" is another activity we like to watch, with a string of prominent drivers on the Formula One and rally circuits.

SISU SPORTING HEROES

True to our *sisu*, Finns thrive in endurance disciplines such as cross-country skiing and long-distance running. Both are rife with *sisu* moments and heroes, from legendary runner Paavo Nurmi (*see* page 126) to skier Juha Mieto. Lasse Virén ran his way into the hearts of all Finns during the 1972 Olympics in Munich when he took a dramatic tumble yet still managed not just to win but set a new world record.

Sports provide an outlet for strong emotions normally kept under wraps. But I think the main reason we are so fond of sports is the promise of *sisu* sightings. We love a good story of winning against all odds, and want to be there when it happens.

DID YOU KNOW?
••••••••••••
Nordic walking – brisk walking with special walking poles – was invented in Finland and suits people of all fitness levels.

THE ABC OF GOAL-SETTING
– how to plan for success

Virtually everyone I've talked to about *sisu* has mentioned the importance of setting goals. You may know what it is you want to achieve – run a race, climb a mountain – but how will you actually go about it? Whatever the aim, planning is key.

To keep your goal from growing too overwhelming and vague, consider the tips below.

A. Set a realistic goal that you believe in

It's fine to have a bold goal, but it needs to lie within the realm of possibility. Once your goal has been set, you need to have patience. Huge accomplishments are often preceded by months or years of work.

B. Split your goal into smaller milestones

In order to reach the end goal, what do you need to do today? Remember to celebrate the milestones, too. If the end goal is being able to run 10km, pat yourself on the back for every kilometre of stamina gained.

C. Prepare, prepare, prepare

It's not enough to keep telling yourself and others that you aren't a quitter. At the end of the day, what makes it possible for you to persevere is having something to fall back on. Sticking to a training plan will give you the assurance you need to keep going when things get tough.

GET MOVING
– some help to get you started

So you would like to improve your fitness, but don't know where to start? You're not alone. Slowly build your *sisu* with these simple steps.

1. EXERCISE WHERE YOU ARE
. . . .

Working out doesn't have to be complicated. Walk or bike to work and take the stairs – *arkiliikunta* is a Finnish concept that simply means to take every opportunity to move, whether you are doing household chores or getting from A to B.

2. SPEND TIME IN NATURE
. . . .

In days gone by, people would run, climb, walk, ski, swim and cycle on a regular basis – without referring to it as a workout. It was simply living life, and something of that ethos remains in Finland today. Take a brisk walk in a nearby forest, wood or park, climb a peak, go berry picking or take that extra leisurely loop around your local lake on the bike.

3. START SMALL
. . . .

Real change is slow. If you are planning to get in shape, don't tell everyone you'll run a marathon next summer. Instead, make it your first goal to run to the end of your street and then build on that – it's the *sisu* way.

DID YOU KNOW?
. . . .

In Finland, lots of road room is provided for pedestrians and cyclists, and a legal proposition was recently made to allow people cycling to work the same tax-deductible benefits given to motorists.

SISU STORY
– Paavo Nurmi, athlete extraordinaire

During the Paris Olympics of 1924, in the five-mile (8km) cross-country running event, temperatures of 45°C (113°F) caused all but 15 of the 38 competitors to abandon the race. Eight were taken away on stretchers. One athlete was so disoriented that he began to run in circles before crashing into the stands and knocking himself unconscious. Spectators were shocked, and Olympic officials banned cross-country running from future Games. Paavo Nurmi exhibited only slight signs of exhaustion after beating countryman "Ville" Eino Ritola to the win by nearly a minute and a half, later crediting the Finnish sauna for his stamina.

Paavo Nurmi (1897–1973) was a celebrated middle- and long-distance runner whose impact on sports and the national psyche in Finland is hard to overestimate.

He set 22 official world records at distances between 1,500m and 20km, winning nine gold and three silver medals in his 12 events in the Olympic Games. At his peak, Nurmi was undefeated at distances from 800m upwards for 121 races. Known for his stern self-discipline and white-hot ambition, Nurmi became something of an archetype of the "strong, silent Finn" for generations to come.

WHY PAAVO NURMI EMBODIES *SISU*

Nurmi emphasized the importance of mental strength. He is famously quoted as saying: "Mind is everything; muscle – pieces of rubber. All that I am, I am because of my mind". Nurmi told a rival runner to forget his opponents: "Conquering yourself is the greatest challenge of an athlete".

As a person, Nurmi has been described as difficult, taciturn and stubborn. Some contemporaries nicknamed him *Suuri Vaikenija* ("The Great Silent One"). Arguably the biggest sporting figure in the world at his peak, Nurmi was nevertheless averse to publicity and despised the trappings of fame. He went on to forge a successful business career.

THREE THINGS TO LEARN FROM PAAVO:

1. Compete only against yourself

The only one to beat is yourself. Living with a mindset of having to race other people is exhausting and will cause you to live in a state of constant tension.

2. The battle is won in your mind

Believing you can overcome any obstacle is necessary. But if you feel you don't have it in you, don't lose heart. Most of us have a damaged self-esteem that needs repairing. Start with introspection. Why don't you believe in your own ability? What steps can you take to build stronger self-belief?

3. Find your strength in silence

I wonder what Paavo would have thought of the connected lives we lead nowadays. He might say it's a world away from how he discovered and honed his inner strength – pounding pavements in silence, mile after mile. Silence is essential to inner focus. Paavo may have left his fellow competitors in a cloud of dust, but he didn't run away from himself.

"Mind is everything."

THE COMFORT ZONE
– and why you sometimes need to leave it

We all have a comfort zone – the mental state that we prefer to live in – and usually spend our everyday lives within this zone, doing things we know we are good at. Comfort zones are healthy, but we need challenges in order to flourish. *Sisu* is rarely needed within the comfort zone, but comes into play as we venture outside of it.

The notion of the comfort zone involves the concept of "optimal anxiety", a low level of stress just outside the comfort zone. Most of us will be familiar with this state of relative unease and discomfort as we face a new demanding situation. When you challenge yourself and tap into your *sisu*, you can achieve amazing results. However, pushing too hard can cause stress levels to soar, often reinforcing the idea that challenging yourself was a bad idea in the first place. Anxiety needs to be kept at a manageable level.

Everyone's comfort zone is different, and what may expand your horizons may paralyze someone else. But stepping outside your comfort zone is what makes your life dynamic.

Feel like you've lingered in the zone too long? Broadening your horizons is actually something you can practise.

1. Do everyday things differently

Take a different route to work. Try a new restaurant. Read something by a new author. Make a change in the way you do things on a day-to-day basis, and see what happens.

2. Take small steps

It takes *sisu* to break out of your comfort zone. Don't be afraid to start slowly. If you're socially insecure, don't try to ask your crush on a date right away – just say hello and go from there.

3. Take time on decisions

Slow down, observe what's going on and take time to interpret what you see. Sometimes just defending your right to make an educated decision can push you out of your comfort zone. Don't just react – think.

WINTER BATHING
– not as extreme as you think

Winter bathing is a Finnish pastime enjoyed mostly by the older generation, but becoming increasingly popular among the young and hip. No longer just about toughening up, the icy dip is valued for its health benefits and incomparable energy boost.

Make no mistake about it: lowering yourself into the freezing-cold water will require a good dose of *sisu*. But once you're past the initial shock, the experience will leave you feeling fantastically refreshed.

MAKING FRIENDS WITH ICY WATER

Swimming in icy water boosts circulation and digestion, and has been proven to slow down ageing and firm the skin. Regulars also experience significant drops in blood pressure. Many people in northern Finland start their mornings this way.

Despite sounding so extreme, *avantouinti* (*avanto* = "hole in the ice"; *uinti* = "swimming") suits virtually everyone. However, if you have heart problems or high blood pressure, consult a doctor first.

THE TRICKS
1. Cool down first

Although people usually go from the sauna to their icy dips, it is important to let the body cool off a little before getting in the water so as to make the temperature contrast less extreme.

2. Warm up your muscles

If you don't start with a sauna, it's a good idea to warm up your muscles with a little exercise.

3. Ease yourself in

Lower yourself slowly into the water and spend just a minute or so in the water the first time. As you get used to it, you'll be able to stay longer, but lingering is not the aim.

4. Breathe

The cold will make you gasp for breath at first, but breathing exercises will help you breathe normally.

5. Wrap up afterward

Once you're out of the water, dry off thoroughly and dress warmly.

SISU STORY
– interview with Patrick "Pata" Degerman

Finn Pata Degerman's business card reads "Explorer". Over the past 20 years he has organized and led over 40 trips to the Arctic and five to unexplored areas of Antarctica, as well as to the Amazonas, Borneo and various uninhabited islands in the Pacific. He has also been the first to scale 16 different peaks around the world. As someone who has faced some of the harshest conditions on the planet and stared death in the face several times, Pata is a firm believer in *sisu*.

"*Sisu* to me means never giving up. And I mean never, ever, *ever*! It's a strength resource to tap into when there is already a conflict going on within you. Things haven't been going your way for a while, and you might be physically or mentally exhausted. I've come close to giving up lots of times. But usually all it takes is half a day of feeling deflated, then I think: 'Am I just going to throw in the towel now, after everything I've been through to get here?' And then I ask myself: 'Is this thing still achievable?' If I can answer in the affirmative, I begin pushing through the obstacles.

"Patience is a key part of *sisu*. Sometimes you have to wait for years to see something happen. It's not the same as stubbornness, though – that can quickly make you impossible to deal with. *Sisu* allows you to be diplomatic and considerate, while also tenacious enough to outlast the competition.

"If you have the concept of *sisu* ingrained in your mind, it helps you rise to the occasion much more quickly. That's the advantage that I really feel we Finns have: not that *sisu* itself is a quintessentially Finnish thing, but that we have named it and learned to tap into it."

PATA'S *SISU* PRINCIPLES TO LIVE BY:

1. Never give up, no matter what!

Although determination is key, it needs to be backed up by good plans and good preparation.

2. Get your motives right

You can then more easily step outside your comfort zone and reach much higher levels than you thought possible. Know why you want to accomplish something, and believe you can do it.

3. Bravery is being afraid and still going on

Having *sisu* is not about not having fear. Fear is a healthy human reaction that can serve us well. Just don't let fear sit in the driver's seat.

4. If you do nothing, nothing will happen

This is as simple as it sounds: pursue your dreams rather than live with regret.

5. If you never ask, you will never get

Few things can be accomplished completely on your own. You need others, and you must not be afraid to ask for help.

DID YOU KNOW?

In 1997, Pata Degerman and fellow mountaineer Veikka Gustafsson were the first to scale a peak in Antarctica that they subsequently named Mount Sisu. On reaching the summit, the pair had been awake for 40 hours straight. In order to avoid getting caught in an approaching storm, they immediately had to begin an arduous 34-hour descent on the safest route, which took them across another two peaks – in temperatures of –60°C (–76°F).

POSITIVE MENTAL ATTITUDE (PMA)
– *sisu* and the science of happiness

Surprisingly little research has been done on *sisu* as a psychological construct. Somehow it's not so surprising: the Finnish sense of modesty can sometimes be a hindrance to recognizing and promoting our strengths. But considering that *sisu* is an attitude that helps us take positive action and stretch beyond our perceived strength, its place in positive psychology ("the science of happiness") is evident.

Related to positive psychology we have positive mental attitude, or PMA. This is the philosophy of adopting an optimistic disposition in every situation, in order to attract positive change and increase achievement. Optimism and hope are vital parts of PMA.

MORE THAN MENTAL

PMA is something of an industry, with self-help books on optimism and the idea that attitudes can be modified through training. That is all well and good, but my gut instinct about *sisu* is that it's not something solely for the cheerfully optimistic. Quite the contrary. We Finns are not exactly famous for our sunny disposition, yet we have identified and implemented *sisu*. This leads us to an interesting question: do you need to think positively in order to be able to tap into *sisu*?

I don't actually think so. I think *sisu* is a deeply felt resource that goes beyond emotion. *Sisu* is not about feeling (or having to feel) the right things. More than something to acquire, it is something to be discovered – a kind of bedrock that is already there. And that is an encouraging thought.

FIGHTING THE GOOD FIGHT

6

From overcoming hardships to becoming a person of integrity (even online), discover the role *sisu* plays in strengthening character and inspiring bravery.

GROWING A BACKBONE
– how *sisu* helps you fight for what you believe in

The world we live in seems to be growing increasingly polarized. Politics are divisive; election results sometimes reveal fault lines that split countries in half. Politics, religion, ideology, the environment – virtually every topic has the capacity to stir emotions and spark opinions. For whatever reason, shades of grey are being asked to give way to stark black and white.

With the global reach of social media, we can share our brilliant insights (ahem) with literally the whole world, at least in theory. Love it or hate it, that's the world we live in. Navigating it with dignity and integrity is becoming increasingly important.

GOING IT ALONE

Sisu gives you the courage to stand alone, if you have to. It makes you someone not daunted by the crowds, someone who doesn't need anyone else's approval in order to do the right thing. Having *sisu* means looking for affirmation not from others but from deep within yourself, your private convictions and perhaps your faith.

"*Sisu* is the reserve fuel tank we didn't perhaps know we had."

STANDING UP FOR YOUR BELIEFS
– cultivating integrity, bravery, respect

Finns are sticklers for abiding by the rules. Being firmly principled is a matter of *sisu*, and "doing the right thing" enables you to keep your head high in all circumstances.

CULTIVATE INTEGRITY

So many of our opinions are inherited and we tend to surround ourselves with people who think like we do, creating bubbles. Still, there is no shortage of information out there to help us make informed decisions.

Things to ask yourself: Are you able to explain your stance to someone who doesn't understand it? What ideas, beliefs or prejudices do you think might be affecting your worldview? Are your opinions written in stone or are you open to changing them?

CULTIVATE BRAVERY

August Landmesser was a shipyard worker in Hamburg, Germany, when the naval ship *Horst Wessel* was launched there to great fanfare in 1936. In a veritable sea of Nazi salutes, he was photographed with his arms demonstrably folded over his chest (*see* left).

This silent resistance took some serious *sisu*. Landmesser would end up spending several years in a concentration camp. He took a risk, and he knew it. But today he is the only person in that group of people who is hailed – for his bravery.

Ask yourself: Are there things I would stand by no matter what? Is there anything that would help me feel more courageous? If so, what?

CULTIVATE RESPECT

Respect is integral to acting with *sisu*. If you only care about your own convictions and will write off anyone who doesn't agree with you, you don't command respect. Respect can't be demanded, only inspired.

Ask yourself: What kind of tone am I using when I debate something – is it respectful and considerate, or condescending and belittling? Am I a good listener? Would I like to discuss something with myself?

SISU STORY
– interview with social activist Emilia Lahti

If Finland has a First Lady of *sisu*, it is Emilia Lahti, a PhD candidate in applied psychology and perhaps the only scholar in the world to focus solely on *sisu*. She is also a social activist and speaker who believes *sisu* can change the world for the better.

Academics aside, Emilia's *sisu* story is a personal one. Her journey toward discovering what she calls "the amazing potential inherent in all of us" started when she left an abusive relationship. A run across New Zealand, a journey of some 1,500 miles (2,400km), forms part of her project *Sisu not Silence*.

HOW DO YOU DEFINE *SISU*?

"The universal ability of humans to stretch beyond their observed limitations and tap into their reserves of embodied strength. *Sisu* is more somatic and visceral than it is cognitive. Take *sisu* versus grit: the latter is defined by passion and is something we use to stay focused and reach a goal. But *sisu* is what gets us past the worst moments. When we feel close to giving up, *sisu* is the second wind that propels us forward."

CAN THERE BE TOO MUCH *SISU*?

"*Sisu* in itself is a neutral tool: what it becomes depends on how we use it. But it's definitely possible to push yourself too hard, to the detriment of your health or those closest to you. We need to always be gracious and remember that we are all just human."

WHAT WOULD YOU LIKE PEOPLE TO UNDERSTAND ABOUT *SISU*?

"*Sisu* is a community thing. We are strong together, first and foremost. It's such a powerful image, that of the lone hero pushing through barriers, but we need a better narrative than that. It's when we are able to inspire *sisu* in each other that it really takes off!"

HOW DID YOUR PROJECT *SISU NOT SILENCE* COME ABOUT?

"I wanted to make a statement about what I had lived through as an overcomer of domestic violence, while also conducting some action research on *sisu*. Running across New Zealand seemed like the most audacious thing I could do!"

GROWING *SISUKAS* – EMILIA'S TOP TIPS:

1. Start with baby steps
. . . .

Our capacity as human beings to rise above difficulty is the sum of many parts, and there is no one-size-fits-all solution to *sisu*. Big goals can be sort of paralyzing, so chop them into manageable parts. Ask yourself: what do I need to do today to reach my goal?

2. Take that first step
. . . .

How often do we let that voice in our head prevent us from starting? So many wonderful endeavours never see the light of day because we are too afraid to try. Ask yourself: What would I do if fear wasn't an obstacle?

3. Reach out
. . . .

In the face of extreme challenge, we all stand naked and in need of support. We all yearn to bask in the light of someone else's kind gaze that says "you can do it". When we learn to understand *sisu* as a universal potential and recognize it in each other – looking beyond all those labels we love to stick on each other such as race, religion, sexual orientation and the rest – I really believe it can help tear down some of the barriers we put up between each other.

"*Sisu* is a verb. It invites you to act, to do, to grab hold of something."

. . . .

DOES SISU MAKE US HAPPY ?

7

Some thoughts on how *sisu* can help us lead the kind of life we want, and some tips to take along as you (hopefully) give it a try.

SISU & HAPPINESS
– some reflections

When I sarted writing this book, I quietly wondered if I was the right person to do it. The image I had in my mind of a person embodying *sisu* was one of those tough, weather-beaten types who pitch a tent in 30mph winds and laugh as icicles form in their beard – people like Pata Degerman (*see* page 134).

I'm decidedly a more cautious type. But if there's one thing I've realized while writing and thinking about this book, it is that *sisu* comes in different forms. Most of us will (hopefully) never have to experience war. The physically brave may choose a life of daring, but most of us opt for a calmer existence. Over a lifetime, however, we will all be climbing our own peaks.

THE POWER OF *SISU*

Does *sisu* make us happy? A difficult question to answer, as it means different things to different people. But looking at what we Finns agree that *sisu* has bought us – freedom, independence, welfare, success – I would say it does. What is happiness if not living the life you have chosen? And *sisu* gives us choice. It allows us to be overcomers.

What I think really testifies to the power of *sisu*, this elusive gut strength, is that Finns are not overcomers by nature. That is to say, our culture is not very optimistic and we do not esteem ourselves very highly – things normally perceived as essential to success.

So let's forget the preconceived ideas. I am a person of *sisu* – and so are you.

GETTING STARTED WITH SISU
– some things to take with you

Whether you want to push through a crisis, improve your fitness, raise resilient kids or have better relationships, you will hopefully have found lots of helpful tips and stories to get you started living a life of *sisu*.

You will also have learned about the quirkiness of Finns and how *sisu* has shaped us as a nation. And even if inspirational talk isn't your cup of tea, I hope the concept of *sisu* has at least intrigued you.

To launch your life of *sisu*, try the following easy steps:

1. Go for a walk in nature

Breathe, be still and dare to really spend some time with yourself.

2. Have that discussion you've been putting off

Taking what you have learned about communicating directly and fairly, schedule in that heartfelt chat.

3. Take the kids on an outing

Dress appropriately, and don't give in to any whining about the weather. Look for your own inner child, too, while you are out there.

4. Set a fitness goal

It doesn't have to be impressive to anyone else. *Sisu* is about doing things for you.

5. Review how you communicate online

What to throw: venomous anonymity. What to grow: integrity and grace.

And who knows? Maybe you'll find yourself looking to your gut for strength a little more often.

MY SISU HERO
– an inspiration

At the beginning of this book, I spoke about trying to find the "main thread" of *sisu*, some clarifying thought to open up the concept. For me, it has turned out to be this: *sisu* is something we inspire in each other.

The person who embodies *sisu* the most to me is my brother. He has a chronic and debilitating disease that affects his muscles, depleting them of all strength from one moment to the next.

My brother has always been very skilled at carpentry, crafting the most beautiful things and working on them until perfect. And after he became ill, he would do the same. His muscles would spasm, but he would take a short break and come back. Or he would just keep going, letting it take five times, ten times as long. He would pick up the tool again and again, patiently working at it even as his body was working against him.

He has quietly exerted his will over the disease, letting it know who is in charge and that he is going to live as much as he can, for as long as he can. And do it bravely. It has broken my heart and made it swell with pride to see it, every time.

His body may be frail, but his spirit is all *sisu*. And it is to him and everyone else out there like him, fighting heroic battles that few people know anything about, that I would like to dedicate this book. *Sisu* may have many facets and many uses, but you are the ones who give it a face.

INDEX (page numbers in *italics* refer to photographs and illustrations)

PICTURE CREDITS

RESOURCES

Page 50: The Finnish Association for Nature Conservation's tips: www.sll.fi/mita-me-teemme/ymparistokasvatus/hyvanmielenpolku

THANK YOU

To the inspiring *sisu* souls featured in this book, for your time, generosity and invaluable insight. To finland.fi and www.visitfinland.com for useful information wrapped in beauty and humour. To Johnny, for your unwavering love and support. And to Adonai, for breathing *sisu* into human hearts.